PERSIAN EMPIRE

A History from Beginning to End

Copyright © 2021 by Hourly History.

All rights reserved.

Table of Contents

Introduction
The Ancient Persian Empires: Achaemenid and Sasanian Empires
The Arab Conquest and the Rise of Islam
The Golden Age of the Persian Empire: The Safavid Dynasty
Art, Religion, and Culture in the Golden Age
The Turbulent Years of the Eighteenth Century
The Qajar Dynasty
Revolutions and Upheaval: The End of the Persian Empire
The Last Dynasty of the Persian Empire
Conclusion
Bibliography

Introduction

The Persian Empire began sometime around 550 BCE, lasting not only centuries but millennia all the way into the twentieth century CE. It existed in the region that we today refer to as the Middle East, specifically headquartered in present-day Iran. Its vast swath of influence and long history make it one of the most prominent societies in human history.

In some ways, the term "Persian Empire" is something of a misnomer, as it is actually a series of dynasties and empires that controlled present-day Iran and surrounding regions. Because the dynasties usually followed one another, and because they occupied the same regions and maintained similar cultures, they are understood to be contiguous. However, important distinctions between them exist, and each established its own government.

While the dynasties were separate, there were very distinct elements that united them, which is a large part of the reason that historians group them together. Persian culture is perhaps the most enduring legacy of the series of empires that occupied Iran. The design and art styles that we largely associate with Persia (as well as present-day Iran) and even Islam were solidified by the Safavid Empire in the 1500s-1700s but have their roots all the way back into ancient times.

Persia has been a major player in an innumerable number of events in the history of humanity. It played a role in some of the most central events of the bible, including the Babylonian exile. It interacted with and influenced the ancient Greek and Roman civilizations, widely considered the foundation of the modern west. It was absolutely instrumental in not only the spread of Islam but also the eventual divisions within the religion. It saw the rise of other powerful empires, especially the British and Russian empires. It was an important location in both world wars. And, it finally succumbed to the revolutionary fervor of the twentieth century, ushering in present-day Iran.

As is clear, the history of the Persian Empire is vast and complex. It has filled many volumes of books, enough to fill entire libraries. This history provides a broad overview, but much more information is available about every person, place, and event discussed herein.

Chapter One

The Ancient Persian Empires: Achaemenid and Sasanian Empires

"The most disgraceful thing in the world, the Persians think, is to tell a lie; the next worst, to owe a debt: because, among other reasons, the debtor is obliged to tell lies."

—Herodotus, ancient Greek historian

The First Persian Empire, also known as the Achaemenid Empire, began around 550 BCE, established by the ruler Cyrus the Great. It was formed from a sort of union between several regional tribes, as well as the conquest of the Median Empire, Lydia, and most notably, the powerful Babylonian Empire. By the end of the 500s BCE, the Persian ruler also served as the pharaoh of Egypt until the empire fell apart about two hundred years later, in the 300s BCE.

The Achaemenid Empire was impressive indeed and helped set the tone for subsequent Persian Empires. At its peak, this empire stretched from North Africa and Eastern Europe to the Indus Valley on the north Indian subcontinent. They created many hallmarks of a truly powerful, advanced civilization that historians use to categorize ancient societies. They built roads, revolutionized farming, established an official language, maintained a powerful military, and even developed a postal system. They also carried water far distances via underwater "qanat" that allowed them to build beautiful gardens, palaces, and farms. They were governed by a single ruler, called the "King of Kings," who supervised a series of "satraps," or provincial governors. Especially for its time, this was a sophisticated and organized government.

The Achaemenid Empire posed a serious threat to their contemporaries, most notably the Greeks, whose empire was flourishing around the same time. Persian Emperor Cyrus the Great conquered some Greek-held territories in the mid-500s BCE while establishing his empire, leading to the Greco-Persian War, a major conflict during ancient times. The Greeks fought a fifty-year campaign—from 499 to 449 BCE—to attempt to win back their former territories.

The Greco-Persian War was made more complicated because these regions were often in rebellion, forcing the Persians to pay close attention. However, despite the importance of this conflict, the outcome remains a historical mystery. Contemporary historians as well as modern historians do not agree on the outcome of the Greco-Persian War. That said, the most likely outcome was some kind of new border established between the two great empires, which both agreed not to cross. There were likely also limits placed on where each could sail.

Not all contact between the Greek and Achaemenid Empires was violent, however. In fact, both influenced each other greatly from a cultural perspective, and some of this cultural exchange took place in part because of the war. Particularly in the city of Athens, trade and cultural exchange flourished. Art historians have established definite connections between surviving artwork of the time from both societies. In addition, each appears to have influenced the other in customs, language, religion, and more. Texts from each civilization have been found among the other, translated into their own languages.

In terms of the things that characterized Achaemenid culture specifically, the Persians in the Achaemenid Empire held their concept of the truth in particularly high esteem. It was considered a grave sin, and even a crime, to lie. This moral outlook guided their religious and secular activities. In addition, they built impressive palaces, cities, mausoleums, and other structures. Just like the Greeks, this ability to develop a unique style and build impressive structures within it is one of their most enduring legacies and a hallmark of their advanced way of life.

Another major historical event in which the Achaemenid Empire was involved was the end of the Babylonian captivity of the Jews. This incident began years earlier when the Babylonian King Nebuchadnezzar captured Judah and destroyed the city of Jerusalem, the seat of Judaism at the time. After the Hebrew ruler refused to pay a tax tribute to Babylon, the Babylonian government exiled many of the Jews from their homeland and destroyed the Jewish temple (the construction of which is a major feature in the Hebrew Bible). All of this happened before the Achaemenids came to power. Once Cyrus conquered

Babylonia, Jews were permitted to return to Judah and build the Second Temple.

Despite their importance and their influence, by the 330s BCE, the empire had started to crumble. The last Achaemenid Persian ruler, Darius III, lost the loyalty of many of the satraps. In addition, Alexander the Great was marching around the known world, successfully conquering many areas and threatening Persian lands. In 330 BCE, he successfully invaded the Persian capital of Persepolis, and the first Persian Empire came to an end.

Another Persian Empire would not rise for more than two hundred years. During that intervening time, the region of Persia was largely controlled by another dynasty known as the Parthian Empire. The House of Sasan—a Persian dynasty—succeeded them, forming the Sasanian Empire, which ruled until after 600 CE. This empire is also referred to as the Empire of Iranians and the Neo-Persian Empire, the last Persian Empire before the spread of Islam in the region.

At their height, the Sasanian Empire encompassed an almost incomprehensible amount of territory. Headquartered in present-day Iran, it controlled what is now Afghanistan, Armenia, Azerbaijan, Bahrain, Dagestan, Egypt, Georgia, Iraq, Israel, Jordan, Kuwait, Lebanon, Palestine, Pakistan, Qatar, Syria, Tajikistan, United Arab Emirates, Uzbekistan, and Yemen. Like the Achaemenid Empire, the Sasanians were also ruled by a "King of Kings," who they called the "shahanshah." The shahanshah oversaw the adjudication of nobility, called "shahrdar," and priests, called "mowbed," in local provinces. However, the government of the Sasanian Empire was very centralized, especially for its time. It also created a vast bureaucracy with a prime minister in which priests had a great deal of power.

These priests were members of the Zoroastrian religion. Zoroastrianism was common in the region before the spread of Islam, and religion was very important in the Sasanian Empire. It was inextricable from the government and military since, by its nature, Zoroastrianism separated all aspects of life into good and evil, with a strong belief in judgment after death and the importance of free will.

Like the Achaemenids before them, the Sasanians had a profound impact on the world around them, developing a distinct culture and making significant strides in government, science, and engineering. They were also important proponents of learning and the arts. They established one of the first major academies in human history, which, within 100 years of its founding, enrolled more than 30,000 students. Sasanians were prolific writers and philosophers and also translated important works from other cultures (most notably the Greeks) into their own language.

Perhaps the Sasanians most important and most enduring influence was on the religion of Islam, even though it had not yet come to Persia at the time. When the people of the region were converted to Islam in the coming centuries, it was within the context of Sasanian culture: not only beliefs and practices but also art, architecture, and rhythms of daily life. Like any young, proselytizing religion, it not only adapted its new adherents to itself but also adapted itself to those people. Many of the artistic and religious hallmarks of Islam have roots in the Sasanian Empire.

In addition, the Sasanians also influenced other peoples and religions. They spread many of their ideas to the Roman Empire, and ongoing warfare between the two helped shape the Roman military structure, which in turn shaped many European armies to come. Some of the Talmud, the sacred Jewish texts, were written during the time of the Sasanians and within or nearby their empire. Also, very early sects of Christianity developed within the Sasanian Empire, and still retain elements of their culture.

The fall of the Sasanian Empire came rather suddenly and was completed by the Arabs and the Islamic caliphate by 651 CE. A combination of factors, including exhaustion of the military from constant warfare with the Romans and Byzantines, an overtaxed population, and other internal disagreements on government and finance all contributed to its downfall. Local Persian communities would at times continue to resist Arab encroachment, but officially, the Sasanian Empire had come to an end by 651.

Like the rise of Christianity in Europe, the rise of Islam in the Persian region and beyond would have an impact on every aspect of life to come. However, the Sasanians also greatly influenced the way that Islam manifested in its region and beyond.

Chapter Two

The Arab Conquest and the Rise of Islam

"Make it easy for him, who cannot pay tribute; help him who is weak, let them keep their titles, but do not give them our kuniyat."

—Arab Caliph Umar

The period of time between the Sasanian and Safavid dynasties may be seen as a kind of break in the Persian Empire. Civil wars erupted across the region, and most importantly, no centralized government existed to unite the vast territory. That said, the period between the two reigns—from about 651 CE until the early sixteenth century—saw important developments that would eventually lead to greater unity.

As previously discussed, the Sasanians were in nearly constant warfare with the Roman and Byzantine Empires, which greatly weakened their resources. This left them vulnerable to outside attack, which is exactly what happened in the seventh century. The conquest of Persia began in 633 and concluded in 651. This was not an easy transition, however; many Persian cities and provinces fought against their initial conquest by the Arabs or rose up in opposition to their new Arab leaders after the fall of the empire.

Certainly, the most important impact that the Arab conquest had on the Persian region was the spread of the Islamic religion. The religion of the Sasanians, and most of the region before the Arab conquest, was known as Zoroastrianism, or Mazdayasna. These terms are broad and encompass a wide range of beliefs, but essentially, it espoused a dichotomous view of all life—material and spiritual—between forces of good and evil. Zoroastrians believed in a final judgment after death, after which individuals would be cast into either heaven or hell. As previously discussed, it impacted every area of life, including government and culture.

The transition between Zoroastrianism and Islam was relatively peaceful, especially in comparison with the spread of other major religions in other regions of the world, most notably Christianity. Islam was a very new religion at the time of the conquest; Muhammad, its founder, was not even born until 570. Thus, while the Arabs were mostly Muslim already, the spread of the religion was largely through evangelism rather than force and happened over the course of centuries. There are instances in some places where Zoroastrianism was outlawed, or Zoroastrians were persecuted, but these were not the norm.

It is difficult to summarize the impact of the era of Arab conquest on Persia since it lasted for so long and the world changed so much during its time. However, besides the spread of Islam, perhaps the other most important influence they had was in their lack of influence, and in their willingness to allow local populations to retain aspects of their own cultures. In other words, the Arabs maintained their own culture and practices, and they largely avoided intermarriage and settled in their own towns or sections of cities. What was more, just as with Islam, they did not generally force their ways of life or views on the Persians. Their main interest in being present in the region was economic; as long as the taxes levied on the Persians were collected, they were content to leave well enough alone.

As a result of this rather hands-off approach, Persians were able to retain a culture and way of life of their own. In addition, they incorporated Islam into their culture uniquely, forever shaping what it would look like around the world but especially in Iran. As previously stated, Sasanian art and culture impacted Islam almost as much as the religion itself impacted them. While it was the same fundamental religion as that practiced by the Arabs, it had its own individual beliefs and rituals. This is one of the ways that the religion of Islam became divided in its early existence.

The Persian culture and people were not without other outside influences during this time, either. During the thirteenth century, the Mongols invaded parts of the Arab empire and surrounding regions. This forced some outsiders to ingratiate themselves with the Persian people, especially Turks and certain groups of Mongols. As a whole, with the growing incursions into their way of life, Persians and those with them became increasingly entrenched in Islam and within their own communities.

The fact that Persians were able to maintain and continue to develop their own unique culture would become very important after the Arab era came to a close. In the sixteenth century, when the Persian Empire was again established and consolidated under Persian rule, this culture, resplendent with its own style of art, architecture, and literature, would flourish.

Chapter Three

The Golden Age of the Persian Empire: The Safavid Dynasty

"The Persians' schools of thought were the true heirs of the great Islamic thinkers of the golden age of Islam."

—Richard Nelson Frye

Perhaps no dynasty had as great an impact on the Persian Empire and the regions it occupied as the Safavids. They came to power in 1501, just years after Europeans had begun their conquest of the Americas, in an era when trade and empire building sparked exploration, discovery, war, and conquest across the globe. During their rule, which came to a final end in 1736, they greatly expanded the territory of the empire, as well as its power, restoring it to its former glory as a chief player in global trade, especially the trade between east and west.

At the beginning of the sixteenth century, when the Safavids first came to power, religion played an inextricable role in the establishment of governmental power, in a way that was similar to Europe's divine right of kings. Therefore, the Safavids claimed ancestors all the way back to Muhammad, his family, and the first Imam of

Islam. However, modern historians have actually traced the family's origins to different regions of the Middle East. By the time of their rule, they were heavily influenced by Turkish culture and language.

Regardless of their origins or influences, the Safavids became the first home rule since the Sasanians almost one thousand years earlier. However, as previously discussed, the Arabs who controlled the region in the intervening centuries did not force their own culture on Persians. In fact, they deliberately kept themselves separate from the Persians. This meant that Persian culture had maintained its own characteristics and practices. Thus, when the Safavids came to power, they stepped into a thriving, unique civilization.

The style of government that they established was rather advanced for the time. Certainly, the Safavids were ruled by a dynastic family headed by a king, but they also created a highly bureaucratized and specialized system of government with checks and balances built in. The administration ensured that specialists governed and advised in decision making in their areas of expertise, and regions were controlled locally by governors or other officials who reported to the central government and king. At the same time, the checks and balances ensured that no person (other than the king) or group became too powerful. The Safavids were also highly skilled at getting to know their constituents; they relocated tribes or used other methods to prevent any kind of unrest in their kingdom. What was more, while the Safavids established and enforced an official religion (Shia Islam), the government itself was relatively secular for the time. The Persian

Empire was largely a meritocracy, meaning that people obtained jobs, roles, privileges, and other benefits based on their demonstrated skill instead of wealth or birthright.

Despite having such a high-functioning form of government, the Safavids were plagued by frequent, almost constant warfare. Often, this warfare was against their Islamic neighbors. These neighbors, especially the Ottomans and Uzbeks, were Sunni Muslims. Therefore, while they technically fell under the same broad umbrella of Islam, they saw themselves as very different (similar to the conflict around the same time between the Christian Catholics and Christian Protestants). This warfare would eventually weaken and destroy the Safavid dynasty. At the apex of their rule, however, the Safavids controlled a vast empire, which encompassed all or part of present-day Afghanistan, Armenia, Azerbaijan, Bahrain, Georgia, Iraq, Kuwait, Pakistan, Syria, Turkey, Turkmenistan, and Uzbekistan. Their dynasty is considered the birth of modern Iran.

One of the Safavids' biggest influences was the mass conversion of Iran to Shia Islam, rather than Sunni, which had dominated during the years of the Arab conquest. Even more specifically, they espoused Twelver Shiism, also called Imamiyyah. This particular branch of Islam holds that there are only twelve Imams, which are the highest order of the religious leaders of the faith, and that the last of the twelve will come again in a sort of prophetic, messianic manner.

This mass conversion was not only important in Iran but is also of monumental importance in the history of Islam itself. Some of the religious conflicts among different sects of Islam have roots in this much earlier dispute. During the Safavid rule, other forms of Islam were generally not tolerated. There was some religious tolerance for other religions, such as Judaism and especially Christianity, but often adherents to different faiths were considered underclass to Shia Muslims.

The end of the Safavid dynasty was gradual and did not have one single cause. Nearby, the Ottoman Empire—a rival of the Persians—became greatly weakened during their rule, largely by their European neighbors. While this should have been a boon for the Persians, instead, it meant that they weakened their military, spending and supporting it gradually less and less, until it left them vulnerable to outside attack. At the same time (and largely in relation to the decline of the Ottomans), the Shahs became complacent and then corrupt, overspending on decadence and alienating the loyalty of the people.

One of the last Safavid rulers was Sultan Husayn. His rule faced many challenges that he and his government were unprepared to handle. First, unrest had grown in the empire, particularly among the Afghans, who rose up in rebellion. He also inherited a climate of religious persecution, in which any non-Shia Muslims faced intolerance and retaliation, and often violence. This included not only Sunni or other Muslims, but also Christians, Jews, and Zoroastrians. This persecution led to violence and conflict throughout the empire. It also weakened a sense of Persian unity and created distrust for the government. The situation was often made worse by ongoing waves of plague outbreaks, particularly in the northern regions of the empire. Many Persian peoples throughout the empire were becoming increasingly displeased with Husayn's lack of decisive action on any of these issues.

Challenges came from outside as well. Persia began losing ships, islands, and coastal territory to Arabs, as well as to pirates. Finally, and perhaps most importantly, Peter the Great of Russia declared war on Persia in 1722. Although the war lasted only a year, Persia was forced to cede very large swaths of land to Russia, drastically shrinking its borders and its influence.

The coming decades and even centuries brought great upheaval for Persia, for a variety of different reasons. Before we discuss its last two hundred years of existence, however, we will look at some of the cultural and artistic achievements that occurred primarily during the Safavid Empire and that are hallmarks of both Persia and modern-day Iran.

Chapter Four

Art, Religion, and Culture in the Golden Age

"The universe is as a parasite of love."

—Vahshi Bafqi, Safavid era poet

Any historian of the Middle East or the Persian Empire, upon being asked, would immediately mention the Safavids' cultural and artistic contributions to the region as one of the most important aspects of their dynasty. This went hand-in-hand with the reestablishment of a truly Persian Empire: they reasserted not only Persian rule but also Persian culture in the entire region.

The fine arts flourished during the Safavid dynasty, and much of the art was reminiscent of the art forms that predominated during the Sasanian Empire, containing elements and influences that had endured nearly a millennia. This was actually one method that the Safavids used to legitimize their control. By harkening back to former Iranian glory, they were demonstrating to the people that they alone were harbingers of the culture and way of life innate to Persians. It helped them win support, as well as unite the region. Much of the art utilized bright colors, and mosaics were very popular.

Architecture was another one of the major cultural contributions made by the Safavids, and many of their structures—especially mosques—are still landmarks today. They not only decorated many of their structures and buildings throughout the empire with lavish artistry, but they also developed innovative techniques in engineering and architecture that were mimicked in Europe and beyond.

Nowhere was the beauty of the empire on display more than the capital city of Isfahan, in present-day central Iran. Much of its splendor is still standing in the form of mosques, parks, and other works of art and architecture. Perhaps the most stunning feature of the city is the Shah Mosque, built in Naghsh-e Jahan Square. It was built specifically to honor Allah by demonstrating the beauty and splendor of the artistic achievements of the Persian people, whom he had blessed. Several minarets surround it, and a uniquely Persian dome stretches skyward. An impressively detailed seven-color mosaic pattern, along with calligraphic designs, frame the walls and ceilings inside. In addition, and in similar beauty, the Safavids sponsored the building of several outdoor parks, some open to the public (the establishment of open public space was not typical during this time), along with libraries that stunned contemporary Europeans.

Other forms of architecture and engineering are also still standing in the city. The Khaju Bridge, more than 400 feet long, features 24 stunning arches. Just as magnificent structures from the Renaissance and early modern period still stand in Europe, there are fabulous vestiges of Safavid Persia in Iran and beyond.

In order to support and encourage the development of scientific and artistic achievements, the Safavids also established schools, where talented individuals received the support necessary to create amazing works, including carpets and other textiles, paintings, sculptures, metalwork, and other works of art. As previously discussed, the Persian Empire was a meritocracy; while imperfect, and while huge advantages were given to children of wealthier families, there were more opportunities for talented individuals in Persia than in Europe.

The Safavids are known for not only sponsoring the arts but for being artists themselves, specifically poets. Shah Ismail I, the first ruler of the Safavid dynasty, composed poetry in both Persian and Turkish. Shah Tahmasp I, his son and successor, was both a poet and a painter. Most of the successive rulers in the Safavid line were also artists of some kind, which reflects the fact that within their kingdom, art and culture were a high priority.

In addition to the arts, the Safavids and their Persian people were also athletes. Especially among the upper classes, archery, wrestling, equestrianism, and other forms of athletic prowess were highly valued. This was also in line with their Islamic beliefs, as taking care of one's body was a high priority.

The artistic and cultural achievements of the Safavid dynasty during this Golden Age of the Persian Empire tells us several things about the era and about the ruling family, besides the fact that they and their subjects possessed great talent. First, prestige was very important to them. It may be surprising to today's world, but mobility was common in the early modern era. Thus, many European and Asian people traveled to and through the Persian Empire, especially traders. The splendor of their cities, both inside buildings and without, told the world that the Safavid dynasty was wealthy and capable of this kind of sponsorship. In addition, it sent a similar message to any potential invaders: the Safavids were powerful, and if they had the resources to invest in this kind of art, their military was even more powerful.

Also, it speaks to the importance of religion and religious unity throughout the empire. Much of this art honored god, or Allah, as evidenced by the fact that the most resources were often devoted to mosques. Finally, this renaissance helped establish the Safavids as legitimate heirs to not only the Persian Empire but also the culture and the people who had protected it from centuries of foreign domination. That the Safavids were such prolific sponsors of this uniquely Persian culture established them as protectors of the past, rightful rulers in the present, and harbingers of the future.

Regardless of their motivations, the artistic, architectural, and cultural achievements of the Safavid dynasty have left modern society with wonders to behold. They are also one of the most important legacies of the dynasty. It impacted all of the Persian dynasties to come and the culture of modern-day Iran, as well as inspiring European and Asian art.

Chapter Five

The Turbulent Years of the Eighteenth Century

*"Unhappy Persia, that in former age
Hast been the seat of mighty conquerors,
That in their prowess and their policies
Have triumphed over Africa and the bounds
Of Europe, where the sun dares scarce appear."*

—Christopher Marlowe

Despite the splendor of the Safavid dynasty, they could not withstand the changes of their more than two centuries of rule. As attention turned away from war and the military and the Shahs became more and more corrupt, other forces stepped in to affect change. First, much of the ruling power previously held by the Shahs was passed to the Shi'a ulama, which was a council of religious authorities. Eventually, they seized power almost entirely and created a kind of Islamic republic based on Qur'anic or Sharia Law.

The final blow to the Safavid dynasty came from the Ghilzai Afghans during the Russo-Persian War. They placed the capital city of Isfahan under siege in 1722. The siege, which lasted nearly eight months, killed an estimated 80,000 residents in the city, mostly from starvation and illness. Finally, Husayn was forced to abdicate and recognize the Afghan leader Mahmud as shah.

After the fall of the Safavid dynasty, the Persian Empire entered years of more upheaval. As the region became more and more incorporated into global trade, economy, and culture, and thus more impacted by world events, never again would the relative calm of the Safavid dynasty occur. Power changed hands more rapidly, territory was lost, fighting increased, and much of the beauty and splendor of the Safavid period ended. However, the Persian Empire remained large, strong, and powerful in many ways.

The dynasty that succeeded the Safavids was the Afsharid dynasty. The Afsharids were Afghani and led the rebellion against the Safavids that overthrew its last Shah. During the reign of the first Afsharid Shah, Nader, Persia regained some of its lost territory and grew even beyond those borders. It was the largest that the empire had been since the Sasanian Empire, and it is important to remember that the world the Sasanians existed in was a very different one. Persia under the Afsharids was very powerful.

This unified glory would be short-lived, however. After Nader's death (he was assassinated during a rebellion against him), the Persian Empire was divided into five major regions, each controlled by a leader from the local ethnic majority. But even this arrangement would not last long; the Afsharids were defeated once and for all in 1796, only about seventy years after their original conquest, by Mohammad Khan Qajar, who would usher in the Qajar dynasty.

At the same time as the Afsharid rule, after Nader's death and the division of the empire, the Zand dynasty ruled simultaneously to the Afsharid. They primarily ruled much of present-day Iran and represented a continual threat to the Afsharid dynasty. Founded by a man named Karim Khan Zand, it saw its zenith under his rule.

In order to legitimize his claim, Karim Khan Zand actually placed an infant descendant of the Safavids on the throne as a figurehead. While he maintained power and technically ruled this region, he spurned the title of shah or king, preferring to refer to himself as "Vakilol Ro'aya," or "Advocate of the People." When viewed in a global context, this decision reflects the growing worldwide discontent with royalty and absolute monarchs. Revolutions instituting representative governments were fomenting and occurring around the world. In addition, it reflected the lack of unity within the Persian Empire itself.

Like the Afsharids, the Zand dynasty was to be short-lived. Karim Khan Shah died in 1779, and much of the empire fell apart after that without him. Even though his family members took over upon his passing, its enemies took advantage of his absence almost immediately, especially the Qajars, who had long been rivals of the Zands. The last Zand ruler was killed by the Qajars in 1794, just two years before the end of the Afsharid dynasty.

Instability dominated throughout the eighteenth century in Persia, as it did in much of the world. Enormous global changes precipitated social changes. However, with the ascendance of the Qajar dynasty, some stability would be restored to the Iranian people and Persia. The Qajars would rule all the way into the twentieth century until after World War I.

Chapter Six

The Qajar Dynasty

"I will rule you differently if I survive"

—Naser al-Din Shah

The Qajar dynasty ruled Persia for more than one hundred years, from 1789 (full control achieved in 1796) until 1925. The family was Persian but from the Turkish region. The world encountered rapid change during this period of time. Persia was both impacted by these changes and contributed to them.

In many ways, the years of the Qajar dynasty marked a period of decline for Persia, especially when taken in comparison to previous dynasties. Chief among the causes was the ongoing war with Russia. The first major conflict was the Russo-Persian War (one of several) of 1804-1813. At this time, both Persia and Russia had new rulers on the throne (Fath Ali Shah Qajar and Tsar Alexander I), both eager to prove their might. Persia had lost territory in present-day Georgia to Russia and wanted it back, while Russia obviously wished to retain it and make further inroads into Persian land.

The war was an uneven match in several ways. First, the Russian troops were greatly outnumbered, mostly because they were also at war with France, Great Britain, the Ottoman Empire, and Sweden at the same time.

However, they enjoyed the advantage of superior supplies and modern techniques of warfare that gave them a critical edge. Even after Persia allied with Napoleon in France and declared a jihad (holy war) in 1810, they were unable to triumph over Russia. They not only permanently lost the regions in Georgia that they sought, but they were also forced to cede Dagestan, comprised of present-day Azerbaijan and parts of Armenia.

The other major conflict during the early decades of the nineteenth century was the Russo-Persian War of 1826-1828. As globalization and alliances grew during the nineteenth century, this conflict had more international factors than the last Russo-Persian War. Great Britain especially played a large role in this war. The British pledged support for Fath Ali Shah and Persia against Russia, but their support would not be enough. The Treaty of Turkmenchay, which ended this war, was even more disastrous than the one ending the 1804-1813 conflict. Persia lost all of its land in the Caucasus, a vast swath of territory that greatly weakened the strength and prestige of the empire. This was also a turning point in that region: Russia was undoubtedly the dominant power. Persia would never again pose a threat to their control of the Caucasus. In fact, it was not until the late twentieth century, with the break-up of the USSR, that these regions emerged from Russian domination.

Thus, the early nineteenth century during the Qajar dynasty saw a period of great decline for Persia, at least in terms of land. Just a few years after this last devastating loss, Fath Ali Shah died, and his grandson, Mohammad Shah, took his place. He devoted his reign to re-gaining some of Persia's former glory, but he was relatively unsuccessful. Even after some resounding victories on the battlefield, his attempts to reform and modernize the military failed, and he died fourteen years after taking the throne.

Mohammad Shah was succeeded by his son, Naser al-Din Shah, and his reign was much more eventful. When he inherited the throne in 1848, the central government of Iran had little control over the tribal communities that dominated the empire. Instead, the members of these tribes (which composed a large amount of the citizenry of Persia) gave their loyalty to local chiefs and religious leaders. Some of them were quite powerful; for example, some were able to raise armies larger than that of the empire itself. They resisted laws passed by the central government, which had virtually no means of enforcement. This made it almost impossible for Naser al-Din to institute any of the changes or reforms that he wished to make, especially at the societal level.

A few years into his reign, though, Naser did take more drastic action to introduce reform across most areas of life in Iran. This largely began with appointing Amir Kabir as prime minister, who was known as a military reformer and immediately began instituting change. From an economic and political standpoint, Kabir was able to balance the then abysmal Iranian budget, as well as levy (and collect) taxes to support his initiatives. He greatly reduced the power of religious leaders, both locally and in the national government. He made strategic infrastructure developments in crucial areas for trade and supported farming of cotton and sugarcane, both enormous cash crops.

From a cultural perspective, perhaps his most important contribution was founding the Darolfonun, Persia's first secondary school. It still exists today, largely as the University of Tehran. This school gave Iranians the opportunity to study arts, humanities, medicine, science, and engineering at home in their own country. He also founded Persia's first newspaper. In addition, he initiated a campaign to vaccinate Iranian children against smallpox, saving many lives. He sought to modernize religion in the country by outlawing practices that he saw as backwards, such as self-flagellation (he had the support of some of the ulema but was ultimately unsuccessful) and promoted religious tolerance of Jews and Christians for the sake of national unity. This all happened in a global context; across the world, nationalism was on the rise and was becoming a more powerful force than religion, tribes, and other loyalties.

The Persian Empire also faced outside challenges during this period. Increasingly, European powers (especially Great Britain) looked to expand their empires into the region. As Britain encroached more and more into India, they wished to secure trade routes (and interrupt those of other powers). This made the land that the Persian Empire occupied incredibly valuable. The ultimate goal of most of Kabir's reforms was creating national unity and a national identity for Iran, which would, in the end, make it better able to withstand these outside encroachments.

Another important aspect of Kabir's time as chief minister was that, unlike many other leaders in history in a similar position, he did not concede to or compromise with his major challengers—Great Britain and Russia. He did not believe that compromise would result in peaceful coexistence; rather, he thought that they would demand more and more concessions until Iran was too weak to fight back. At that point, foreign powers would take over. Therefore, he took a very hard line against both and attempted to form alliances with other nations, primarily their rivals. This foreign policy tactic was very unique and innovative for its time. What was more, he also started a complex web of spies within both Britain and Russia and the people they had in Iran.

As his brief term wore on, however, Amir Kabir fell out of favor with the Shah, for a variety of reasons. First, his reforms were unpopular with some members of the upper class, and especially with the ulema. In addition, Naser al-Din disagreed with some of his approaches and feared that he was becoming too powerful (especially his sway over the military). He saw Kabir as a threat to his power, rather than a source of support. Naser had Kabir exiled and then finally executed in 1852.

After the assassination of Amir Kabir, Iran's movements toward a more modern, westernized country also largely waned. In the coming years, Naser would make decisions that actively undid many of Kabir's reforms. He granted several wildly unpopular concessions to European powers as he became more entrenched in Europe itself, visiting several times and associating with members of European royal families.

As discontent with Naser grew, so did unrest and political action against him within Iran. By the late nineteenth century, groups that recruited thousands of Iranians organized against him and actively opposed his decisions through a variety of means. One of the most influential leaders of these movements was Jamal al-Din al-Afghani, also referred to as Al-Afghani. Al-Afghani traveled throughout the Middle East, Europe, and the Indian subcontinent during his lifetime. He was an Islamic modernist. While Islamic Modernism has many complex aspects, Al-Afghani's main goals were to overcome infighting within the Muslim faith and form unity based on the major tenets that all the sects shared.

Al-Afghani, as an Islamic modernist, also believed that the religion of Islam needed to be reconciled with more modern ideas of life and government, including forming representative governments, tolerance for other religions, civil rights, et cetera. To him and those who thought like him, this was the only way that the Islamic world would survive against the increasingly fierce encroachments by the western world, especially Europe and the United States. Al-Afghani was also associated with a man named Mirza Reza Kermani. In 1896, the two collaborated on a plan to assassinate the Shah. They were successful on May 1.

In the end, in some ways, Amir Kabir was ultimately successful in his endeavors, despite his ignominious end. The collective action taken against the Shah's decisions and in favor of Islamic modernism helped form a sense of Iranian national identity and unite the Persian people. And that, after all, had been Kabir's ultimate goal. Mirza Reza Kermani, the Shah's assassin, was executed, but there was no turning back from the road which Iran had begun to walk. The events of the late nineteenth century and the growing disconnect between the Qajar dynasty and the people of Iran would eventually lead to the Iranian Constitutional Revolution.

Chapter Seven

Revolutions and Upheaval: The End of the Persian Empire

*"I've reached the end of this great history
And all the land will fill with talk of me
I shall not die, these seeds I've sown will save
My name and reputation from the grave,
And men of sense and wisdom will proclaim,
When I have gone, my praises and my fame."*

—Ferdowsi

Life and government in Persia were forever changed by the events of the late nineteenth century. Despite this, even after Naser al-Din Shah's assassination, a Shah from the Qajar family still governed Iran. Naser's son, Mozaffar ad-Din Shah took the throne, and reigned from 1896 to 1907. It was during this time that the Iranian Constitutional Revolution occurred.

The Constitutional Revolution, understood as the first Iranian Revolution, can be seen as a sort of beginning of the end for the Persian Empire. The forces that brought both about were largely the same: growing nationalism and national identity within Iran, coupled with a desire for a more modern, republican style of government.

Mozaffar inherited many of the problems of his father. Iran was still not financially sound, and rather than institute reforms that would strengthen the economy, he instead continued to grant concessions to foreign powers to the intense ire of many Iranian people. In addition, he and his aristocratic counterparts lived lavish lifestyles, further alienating them from the people. By 1905, the Persian people had enough. Mozaffar had borrowed an extravagant amount of money against the Iranian economy in order to finance his personal European tour, and protests broke out. As the government tried to take action against the activists, their ranks only swelled, especially in Tehran. Many allied with religious leaders, taking refuge in mosques or holy cities.

Mozaffar relented in early 1906 and formed a sort of precursor to what would become a parliamentary body. But protests continued, and violence against protesters also erupted. Mozaffar then agreed to create a formal parliament in August of that year, and elections were held. Just before he died, he signed the constitution that solidified the power of the National Consultative Assembly and limited the power of the Shah.

This victory would prove to be short-lived, however, as Mozaffar's son, who became the next shah, undid many of these reforms, re-sparking revolution. Muhammad Ali Shah greatly increased the influence of both Britain and Russia in Iranian affairs, further complicating Iranian politics. He rendered the constitution null and void and launched a counterattack on the activists. However, the activists fought back valiantly and were able to take Tehran in July of 1909. After their victory, Muhammad Ali Shah fled Persia and abdicated the throne.

The leaders of the revolutionaries, known as the Majilis, did not immediately do away with the shah. For one thing, they did not necessarily have the power to do so, and what was more, doing so may have prompted an invasion of Iran by Great Britain, Russia, or both. So, they agreed to place Muhammad Ali's young son on the throne. At only six years old, Ahmad Shah became the last of the Qajar dynasty to hold that title.

A child that young was obviously not old enough to lead a country and certainly did not inspire confidence in the people. However, the constitution was re-instated, and unrest was generally quelled, at least for the time being. But World War I was on the horizon, and while barely a teenager, somehow Ahmad was supposed to lead. World War I rocked Iran. They officially declared neutrality, but their strategic location made it virtually impossible to avoid conflict. Britain occupied vast expanses of their land.

Largely because of the British occupation (and taking place primarily within British-held territory), a devastating famine occurred during the latter years of the war, between 1917-1919. It came to be known as the Great Famine, and it killed more than two million Iranian people. In the years before it broke out, after the start of World War I, the price of wheat and other food staples increased exponentially. Then, years of drought (particularly in 1916) devastated supplies and drove prices even further up. What was more, British and Russian forces both blocked major roadways throughout the region, making it virtually impossible for foodstuffs from elsewhere to be transported.

As the scarcity of food spread, the Iranian people became more desperate. Theft and violence surrounding the acquisition of food became common. The poor especially rose up against law enforcement and other figures of authority. To make matters worse, largely because of the famine, disease also spread rampantly. Of the estimated two million civilian dead, many succumbed to cholera, typhus, and the insidious 1918 outbreak of influenza.

By the time the war ended, Iran—which had officially remained neutral—was rocked by violence and deprivation. It joined much of the rest of the world in the post-war upheavals of 1919, which called for greater workers' rights, more representative governments, and protections for the poor and vulnerable. Just a few years after the end of World War I, Iran had a new ruling dynasty.

Chapter Eight

The Last Dynasty of the Persian Empire

"I heard the voice of your revolution. Let all of us work together to establish real democracy in Iran. I make a commitment to be with you and your revolution against corruption and injustice in Iran."

—Mohammad Reza Shah

The last of the dynasties of the Persian or Iranian Empire was the Pahlavi dynasty, which held power from 1925 until 1979. In 1979, the Iranian Revolution (also known as the Islamic Revolution) occurred, which saw the overthrow of the Shah (who was supported by the United States) and the establishment of a republican government and the Ayatollah.

Unlike the passage between some of the previous Persian dynasties to another, the rise of the Pahlavi dynasty was not peaceful. It formally began in 1925 but really had its roots much earlier. As previously discussed, the Persian people had suffered greatly during World War I and the decades prior. They were deeply unhappy with the Qajar dynasty.

First, a division of the military known as the Persian Cossack Brigade executed a successful coup d'état, overthrowing Ahmad Shah's government (but not necessarily the Shah himself) and taking control of the country. They were led by Reza Khan, who took his orders largely from the British (among other interests, the British feared a socialist or Bolshevik contingent would take control of Iran first). Even though the results were dramatic, the coup itself was not. The sitting government surrendered rather quickly after very little violence.

Reza Khan would eventually become the first Shah of the Pahlavi dynasty, but not immediately after the overthrow of the government. A man named Zia-eddin Tabatabaee served as prime minister, technically still under Ahmad Shah of the Qajar dynasty. While he set lofty goals for his administration, including land redistribution for the poor, he was largely unable to accomplish anything. Eventually, Ahmad Shah removed him from office. Throughout the year, unrest and even uprisings continued to occur throughout Persia, causing almost constant crises and upheaval for the government. In 1923, Reza Khan was named prime minister. That same year, Ahmad Shah left Iran for good; he died in 1930 in Paris. In 1925, the Iranian constituent assembly named Reza Khan the new shah, officially deposing Ahmad Shah and ending the Qajar dynasty.

Reza Shah ruled Iran until 1941. During his time, he made sweeping reforms that forever changed the region and nation. For one thing, he officially named the country Iran instead of Persia. While subsequent Pahlavis would roll this reform back, it was during Reza Shah's rule that the world began referring to the country as Iran more and more.

Reza Shah also set about to modernize his country. At this time, modernization was largely synonymous with westernization; in other words, he wanted Iran to look, feel, and act more like a European nation. He made real, tangible reforms, such as initiating building projects to construct roads, railroads, and other infrastructure. He revolutionized the oil industry, as Iran is a very oil-rich nation, and allowed them to export much more oil than they ever had before. This also provided an economic boon, since oil was in such high demand in the twentieth century. It provided Iran with a bargaining tool as well when dealing with other countries. He also established the University of Tehran, offering advanced study in many fields to Iranians at home.

From a social perspective, other important changes occurred during Reza Shah's rule. The women's movement had begun around 1910 and was still ongoing at this time. Under Reza Shah, women made advancements in education, granting them new access to opportunities and careers. He also sponsored the Second Congress of Eastern Women in 1932, which brought together women's rights activists from Iran and other Middle Eastern countries. Finally, he did away with the wearing of the traditional Islamic garb for women, called the hijab, which covered them from head to toe. This was a highly controversial decision that pitted him against many religious leaders.

In addition to women, Jewish people also gained more rights during Reza Shah's rule. For the first time in a long time, Jews were allowed to hold professions previously exclusive to Muslims. They were also allowed to integrate into neighborhoods and workplaces from which they were previously barred. While anti-Jewish sentiment remained a major issue in Iran, and in no way were Jews equal in Iran to Muslims, these were major steps forward.

It can be difficult to place judgment on these reforms and categorize them as either good or bad. On the one hand, Iran was more capable of participating in global politics and on the global marketplace. Undoubtedly, positive change came for Jews and women as well, although the disappearance of the hijab was problematic for some women, who simply stopped appearing in public rather than be seen without it. Additionally, at the same time, traditional groups were shunned. Reza Shah even forbade photographers from taking pictures of people, places, and practices that he perceived as backwards. In some ways, these reforms turned Reza Shah and Iran away from their traditional background and heritage.

Reza Shah also did not support a democratic government. While parliament remained in session, Reza Shah made sure that elections were arranged so that only those who supported him and his military regime served. He eliminated officials who disagreed with or opposed him and sometimes used violence to quell opposition. He enjoyed tremendous support from both the military and the government bureaucracy. In his creation of a more modern state, tens of thousands of jobs were created. These were handed out just as much as patronage in exchange for loyalty as they were for merit. Thus Reza Shah built himself a powerful network of support.

Not everyone was happy with his reign. Interestingly, the most conservative and most progressive Iranians were unhappy during this time. He greatly alienated the clergy and devout Muslims. He required almost everyone to wear western clothing, which eroded some Islamic traditions. In awarding women's rights, he also allowed women and men to mix in settings that conservative Muslims disapproved of. These disagreements came to a head in 1935, when several activists took refuge in a Muslim shrine. Rather than respect the sacred space, Reza Shah used the military to break through and kill many detractors. This was a permanent break between the Shah and the religious community.

Reza Shah worked to eliminate not only religious diversity in Iran but diversity of almost any kind. He instituted the forced break up of tribes, destroying centuries of tradition. He very much wanted a homogenous culture in Iran and advocated ethnic nationalism, a single, official language, and other aspects of what he deemed a modern society.

Reza Shah led Iran all the way until World War II and the Anglo-Soviet invasion. Just as Persians had long feared, both of their primary foreign threats invaded at the same time. The Soviet Union had only recently allied with Great Britain when they were invaded by Nazi Germany. Both feared that Iran and Reza Shah were sympathetic to Hitler and Nazi Germany and might eventually enter the war on the Axis side. Therefore, they planned Operation Countenance to invade Iran at three points at the same time, further straining Iran's weaker and poorly equipped military.

The invasion took place on August 25, 1941, and was over in just five days, when Iran surrendered. Great Britain and the Soviet Union protected their interests by protecting supply lines (primarily into the Soviet Union) and controlling Iran's rich oil fields, a vitally important commodity in the war. Less than a month after the invasion, Reza Shah abdicated. He died in exile in 1944. His son, Mohammad Reza Shah, took control after him; the British conceded to allowing his son to take over on the condition that Reza Shah left Iran.

Mohammad Reza Shah came to power at a critical time for Iran, and his term on the throne would certainly be eventful. He would reign until 1979 when the Iranian Revolution erupted.

In some ways, Mohammad Reza Shah was like his father and shared some of his goals. Chief among these was the desire to modernize Iran. Thus, with the end of World War II, he set about building infrastructure, developing industry, and growing the military. In many ways, he was successful. Iran's wealth grew exponentially during his reign—not only the country itself but also individual families, who saw their average income multiply more than 400 times. He granted women's suffrage and revolutionized both education and health care in Iran, which he believed were hallmarks of an advanced society. Finally, he was successful in advancing the military; by 1979, Iran had the fifth-largest military in the world.

Mohammad Reza Shah was not popular with all Iranians, however, and his legacy is troubled, to say the least, and is tied in many ways to his alliances with Great Britain and the United States during the Cold War. He was notorious for his severity against his opposition, jailing and torturing his political opponents. He abolished an opposition party and misused his intelligence agency to spy on its own citizens. This not only alienated him from many of the people, especially the poor and people on the political left, but the clergy as well. While his father's modernizing efforts had also certainly created distance between the Pahlavi dynasty and the Islamic leadership, Mohammad Reza Shah solidified it.

During Mohammad Reza Shah's reign in the mid and late twentieth century, oil became a more and more precious commodity across the world. However, Iran was not in control of its oil industry. It was controlled by Great Britain, who had made massive investments in years past to drill, refine, and distribute it. In the early 1950s, Iranian Prime Minister Mohammad Mosaddegh attempted to nationalize the oil industry, which would have brought it back under Iranian control. However, in order to protect Britain's interests, the United States' Central Intelligence Agency orchestrated a coup d'état to remove Mosaddegh from office. While the involvement of the U.S. and the U.K. was largely secret in the west, it was well known in Iran, making it one of the major events that alienated many Iranian people from both countries and their ideologies, which would result in a permanent break after the Iranian Revolution.

Throughout Mohammad Reza Shah's reign, conditions continued to deteriorate for many Iranian people. The Shah's brutal efforts to quell unrest continued, even as his people became more and more disillusioned with him and with the monarchy in general. Finally, in January 1979, the Iranian Revolution broke out. Mohammad Reza Shah surprisingly offered little resistance to the revolution and fled the country. Ruhollah Khomeini, also known as

Ayatollah Khomeini, became the leader of the new Islamic republic of Iran.

After Mohammad Reza Shah fled, fighting continued between rebels and military officials. Many disagreed on what direction Iran should take. However, on February 11, 1979, the Iranian monarchy was officially abolished. More than 2,500 years of the Persian Empire had come to an end.

Conclusion

It is impossible to understate the influence that the Persian Empire has had on the Middle East and on world history. Perhaps that goes without saying since it stretched for more than 2,500 years. Their very presence in the region shaped not only how they developed but the rest of the world as well.

The strategic location of the Persian Empire made it a major player in world events, beginning in ancient times. As discussed herein, the Persians greatly impacted both the Greek and Roman Empires, which in turn left indelible marks on the development of European nations. In both the ancient and modern worlds, Iran is strategically located at a crossroads for world trade, making it a major player in international relations and globalization. Finally, in the twentieth century, its oil reserves have made it a valuable ally and perilous enemy for many.

Certainly, one of the most important legacies of the Persian Empire is the spread of Islam, as well as some of the divisions within that religion. The Arab conquest brought Islam to Persia, but Iranians made it uniquely their own, sowing seeds of division that would later erupt around the world between Sunni and Shia Muslims.

The Persian Empire also helped establish the artistic styles of the Islamic world. These patterns actually began long before the rise of Islam, primarily during the Sasanian Empire. The mosaic tile patterns, minarets, domed mosques, archways, and other features are still closely associated with Islam today.

Again, it is hard to overstate the importance of the Persian Empire, at any point throughout its long history. The identity of the people who would come to call themselves Iranian have one of the longest and richest histories in all humanity.

Bibliography

Amanat, Abbas (2019). Iran: A Modern History.

Daryaee, Touraj. (2013). Sasanian Persia: The Rise and Fall of an Empire.

Kennedy, Hugh. (2008). The Great Arab Conquests: How the Spread of Islam Changed the World We Live In.

Kinzer, Stephen. (2008). All the Shah's Men: An American Coup and the Roots of Middle East Terror.

Martin, Vanessa. (2018). The Qajar Pact: Bargaining, Protest and the State in Nineteenth-Century Persia.

Newman, Andrew J. (2008). Safavid Iran: Rebirth of a Persian Empire.

Olmstead, A.T. (1959). History of the Persian Empire.

Streusand, Douglas E. (2010). Islamic Gunpowder Empires: Ottomans, Safavids, and Mughals.

Waters, Matt. (2014). Ancient Persia: A Concise History of the Achaemenid Empire, 550-330 BCE.

Printed in Great Britain
by Amazon